Discovering Dinosaurs

Pippa Goodhart

Collins

Contents

Bonus: Timeline 2

Chapter 1 Where to find a dinosaur 4

Bonus: Mary Anning 14

Chapter 2 What is a dinosaur? 16

Bonus: Spot the dinosaur! 26

Chapter 3 Following the clues 28

Bonus: Become a fossil-finder! 38

Chapter 4 Different kinds of dinosaur 40

Bonus: Be a footprint detective 48

Chapter 5 When and why did
   dinosaurs die out? 50

Chapter 6 Can we bring dinosaurs back? . . 58

Glossary 68

About the author 70

Book chat 72

BONUS Timeline

Million years ago	New animal or plant
	sea creatures (ammonites)
450	
	fish
434	
	land plants
410	
	trees
354	
	reptiles and winged insects
250	
	dinosaurs and mammals
205	
	many new dinosaurs and birds
141	
	flowering plants
66	★ worldwide extinctions
23.8	
	first humans
1.8	
	early humans
315 thousand years	modern humans

Chapter 1
Where to find a dinosaur

We're going on a dinosaur hunt! Where might we find some?

It's easy to find dinosaurs, but have you ever seen a real living dinosaur? No. Why not? Because dinosaurs lived long before humans existed.

Dinosaurs of various kinds lived on Earth for over 170 million years! They became **extinct** about 66 million years ago. Humans came along tens of millions of years after that.

Even though we can't time travel to see dinosaurs alive, we *can* see remains of actual dinosaurs in museums.

You might wonder how any dinosaur remains could last for tens of millions of years.

Well, they lasted by turning into hard stone fossils.

For thousands of years, people have found fossils. But, for most of that time, they didn't know about dinosaurs. So, they had to guess what animals the fossils had come from.

If you had to guess, what would you think this fossil skull was?

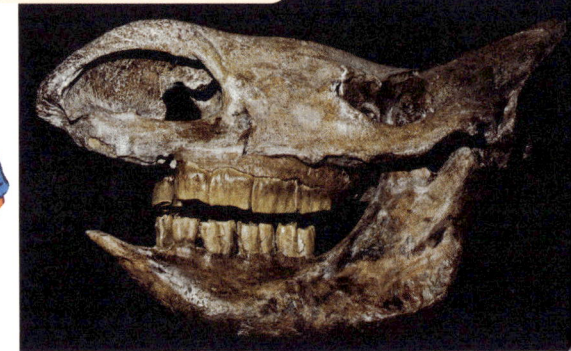

A dragon? That's what the people who found the skull 700 years ago guessed. They even constructed a model dragon to fit their ideas.

Actually, the skull is from a prehistoric woolly rhino.

Thousands of years ago, Greek people made up stories about a sort of giant called a cyclops. These giants had just one eye in the middle of their heads.

What gave them the idea of one-eyed giants?

They had found fossil skulls like this one.

They were actually fossils of prehistoric dwarf elephants. The hole in the front of their heads was where the elephant's trunk came out!

So, even when they found fossils, people didn't always guess correctly!

About 200 years ago, people began sharing their fossil finds, and their ideas. They began to work out more about the animals that left behind the fossils.

At this time, a family called the Annings lived near sea cliffs which were rich in fossils. They hunted for fossils when winter storms washed away parts of those cliffs.

The Annings cleaned their fossils, laid them on a table in front of their house and sold them. Seaside visitors loved the fossil 'curios'.

Can you guess why they called them curios?

It was because the fossils made people curious about what sort of creatures the fossils had once been.

Most of the fossils found by the Annings were parts of small **marine** creatures.

Marine fossils are quite easy to find because there are so many of them.

Ammonites were sea animals with a coiled shell. People called ammonite fossils 'snake stones'.

ammonite

Belemnites were a sort of squid. People called belemnite fossils 'devils' fingers'.

belemnite

But in 1811, the Anning children, Joseph and Mary, spotted something extraordinary. They uncovered an enormous skull, 1.2 metres long.

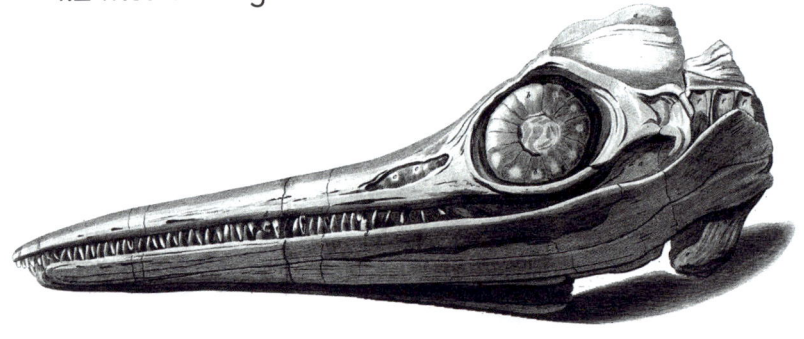

 What animal would you guess this skull came from?

At the time, everyone thought it was a crocodile skull, but it wasn't.

For months, Mary gently chipped away to show more of the fossil creature. What she found was a fossilised body that looked more like a dolphin than a crocodile.

Mary's fossil creature was first exhibited in the British Museum as a 'crocodile in a fossil state'. But then experts at the museum gave it a new name – Ichthyosaurus. You can see it in the Natural History Museum in London!

Fact

Mary also studied coprolites. These look like stones but are actually fossilised poo! By studying these, experts can see what dinosaurs had eaten!

Mary Anning showed that children can be good fossil hunters. Since then, more children have made exciting discoveries.

In 2020, a 12-year-old boy in Canada – Nathan – was exploring a ravine with his dad. Suddenly, he saw a very large fossil bone poking out of the side of the ravine.

Nathan and his dad shared their amazing find with dinosaur experts. Those experts carefully dug out more fossil bones, and a skull.

Nathan had found a young duck-billed dinosaur called a hadrosaur! It had died 69 million years ago.

fossilised bones of a hadrosaur

Nathan's hadrosaur is a dinosaur. But Mary's ichthyosaur is not a dinosaur. Find out why in the next chapter!

a duck-billed hadrosaur

BONUS
Mary Anning

Mary Anning made great fossil discoveries during her lifetime, and she started very young.

Mary's father, Richard, liked to collect fossils. By the time Mary was around five years old, she was out helping him.

This is a painting of Mary Anning as an adult. Can you see what she's pointing at?

This statue of Mary shows her hurrying towards the cliffs with her hammer, and her basket to put her fossils in. She has her companion dog Tray with her.

Did you know?
The rhyme, 'She sells seashells on the sea shore' was about Mary Anning.

Chapter 2
What is a dinosaur?

In 1842, a distinguished Victorian scientist called Richard Owen invented the name 'dinosaur'. He made the name up from two Greek words meaning 'terrible' (dino) and 'lizard' (saur). So, dinosaur means 'terrible lizard'.

Richard Owen

Richard Owen worked with animals at London Zoo, studying their skeletons. Knowing about modern animal bones helped him to understand dinosaur fossil bones better.

He had some full-sized models made. This model shows what he guessed a Megalosaurus would have looked like.

The picture below shows what we *now* think a Megalosaurus looked like.

Can you spot the differences?

Richard Owen thought that a Megalosaurus would have walked on four legs, and he also thought it had a hump on its back. We now know that they walked on their two back legs – as all meat-eating dinosaurs did.

Richard Owen wanted everybody to share his passion for dinosaurs. He helped set up the Natural History Museum in London, in 1881.

Did you know?

The Natural History Museum has fossils from 157 different kinds of dinosaurs. The earliest ones were alive about 240 million years ago. The latest ones were alive about 66 million years ago.

In 2014, the Natural History Museum exhibited the most complete Stegosaurus skeleton ever found. The Stegosaurus has been given the name 'Sophie'.

'Sophie' the Stegosaurus

Fact

Dinosaur fossils have been found on all seven **continents**.

The ichthyosaur and dinosaur names both end in 'saur', meaning 'lizard'. The 'ichthyo' bit of the name means 'fish' in Greek. So, an ichthyosaur was a 'fish lizard'!

Ichthyosaurs were marine creatures, so they never left the sea. But Richard Owen decided that only creatures who lived on the land should be called 'dinosaurs'. This means that Mary Anning's ichthyosaur technically didn't count as a dinosaur.

There's also another reason why ichthyosaurs are not dinosaurs. Victorian scientists were wrong to call ichthyosaurs 'lizards'.

They were wrong because lizards and other reptiles all lay eggs, but ichthyosaurs didn't lay eggs. Ichthyosaur babies grew inside their mothers and were fed with their mother's milk.

That means that ichthyosaurs were mammals, like humans. They weren't reptiles.

Dinosaur babies developed inside eggs, as snakes, turtles, crocodiles and bird babies do. Baby dinosaurs hatched out of the eggs. As soon as they hatched, they started eating food straight away.

Victorian scientists were right to think that dinosaurs *developed* from lizards, but they actually weren't lizards anymore.

Therizinosaurus dinosaur eggs in a nest

You can distinguish a dinosaur from a lizard by the shape made by their hips and legs.

Lizards' legs stick out from their bodies.

Dinosaurs' legs went straight down from their bodies.

Some dinosaurs walked on four legs, and some walked on two legs. But all dinosaurs had legs that went straight down.

So, the 'lizard' part of the 'dinosaur' label is wrong.

Some dinosaurs have 'rex' as part of their name. Everybody has heard of the Tyrannosaurus rex, often called T-rex.

'Rex' is the Latin word for 'king'. Scientists called the T-rex 'king' because it was so enormous and scary they thought it must be the most powerful of all dinosaurs.

Fact

A dinosaur nicknamed 'Scotty' is the largest T-rex skeleton found so far. It is 13 metres long. The shape of the bones suggest that Scotty was female (so a queen, not a king!). Scotty was not yet fully grown.

Some dinosaur names include the word 'raptor'. 'Raptor' is another Latin word. It means to 'seize violently' or 'drag away'. Present-day birds of prey, such as owls and eagles, who kill and eat animals, are raptors. Dinosaurs with 'raptor' names, such as Velociraptor and Microraptor, would eat other animals and birds.

Microraptor

Velociraptor

Why did dinosaurs have Greek and Latin names?

It's because, in the past, these languages were the main languages used in science. However, here is a dinosaur found in 2004 with a Chinese name.

A Yinlong dinosaur. Its name means 'dragon'.

More and more new dinosaurs are being found in Asia. Dinosaur names are becoming more varied, but there aren't yet any dinosaur names in English.

BONUS
Spot the dinosaur!

Erythrosuchus – an early kind of crocodile. Not a dinosaur.

Anchiornis – an early bird, two-legged, with wings. Yes, it IS a dinosaur!

Dimetrodon – looks like a dinosaur and its name sounds like a dinosaur name, but it isn't one. Its legs are wrong for a dinosaur – they don't go straight down. It also lived 40 million years before the first dinosaurs.

Temnodontosaurus – its name sounds dinosaurish, but this is a marine mammal, not a dinosaur.

Chapter 3
Following the clues

We can't study living dinosaurs because they've all gone. So, we must become detectives, using the clues they've left behind.

We have fossil bones and fossil teeth. And those fossils can tell us even more about the dinosaurs than you might guess.

For example, the position of a fossil skeleton, and where it was found, can give us clues about how the creature died.

This baby oviraptorosaur is still curled up in its egg. It died before it could hatch.

These T-rex bones show teeth marks. Because no dinosaur was bigger or stronger than a T-rex, experts think the teeth marks must have been made by another T-rex. They think that T-rexes might have been cannibals, eating each other!

Or maybe they were just battling to be the top T-rex?

29

Often dinosaur skeletons are squashed, scattered or have some bones missing.

Experts can sometimes put the bones back together and make fake bones to fill gaps. That's how the complete dinosaur skeletons in museums are made.

This Triceratops skeleton has been completed and posed to look as though it's about to fight.

When a dinosaur skeleton is put back together, experts can study the whole body. They can then work out how the animal moved, and how fast.

Experts can look at the layer of soil or rock that the fossil is found in to work out how old it is.

And now experts have another way to work out how old the dinosaur was when it died. They put a tiny section of fossil bone under a microscope. As with tree stumps, you can count growth lines, one for each year of life.

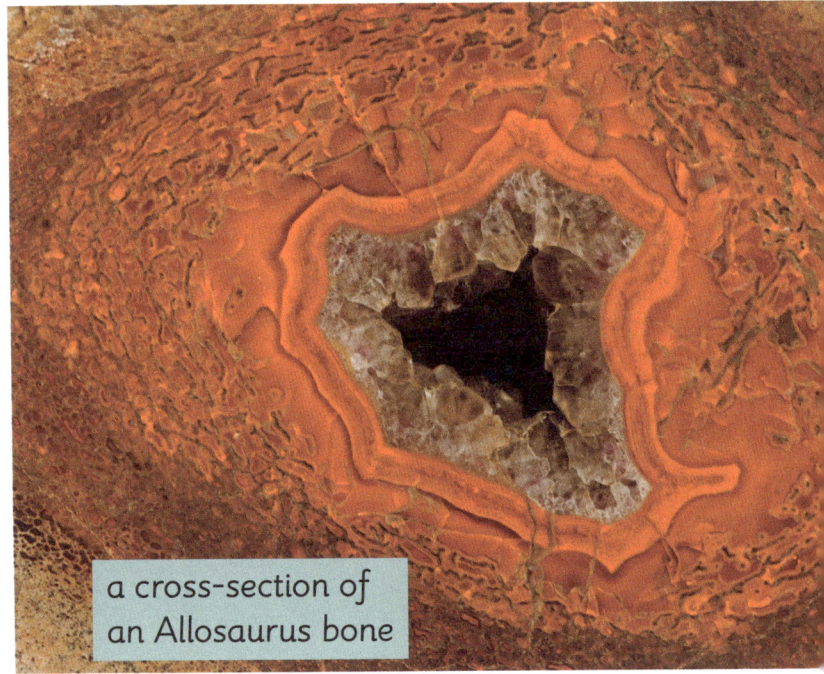

a cross-section of an Allosaurus bone

X-ray scanning lets us see inside a solid fossil. The scan might reveal teeth inside a skull. We can get lots of clues from fossilised dinosaur teeth. For example, the teeth can show us what sort of food that dinosaur liked to eat.

| Meat-eating dinosaurs had sharp teeth, good for seizing their prey and killing it. | Plant-eating dinosaurs had flatter teeth, for pulling at plants and chewing them. |

A four-year-old girl in Wales found a very rare, fossilised dinosaur footprint. Lily spotted it on a rock on a beach. Her parents contacted a museum.

Experts said that the fossil showed the footprint of a small Grallator dinosaur. It had walked on two hind legs, hunting for small animals and insects to eat.

That little dinosaur had made the footprint about 220 million years ago.

Footprints aren't the only kind of fossilised prints dinosaurs left behind. Prints of dinosaur skin and even feathers have been found, although this is very rare.

Here's a fossilised imprint of Triceratops skin. Triceratops lived on plants and travelled in herds.

Previously, experts had no idea that dinosaurs had feathers, but now we know that some of them did.

Both a tiny tick and a dinosaur feather have been **preserved** in this piece of amber for 99 million years!

feather

tick

Did you know?
Amber is sticky **resin** from trees that goes hard when it dries. Over millions of years, that resin turns into stone.

However, very few of the dinosaurs who lived all those millions of years ago have left any clues at all. Experts estimate that only one bone in every billion was fossilised.

What?! Why only one bone in a billion?

It's because most dead animals and birds get eaten or rot away. Nothing is left of their bodies to be fossilised.

Fossils only form in very particular conditions. The dead body has to be covered quickly in mud, ash or **silt** so that air can't get in. Without air, the body doesn't rot. It stays preserved for millions of years as a fossil.

It's estimated that 99% of all fossils are of marine creatures because the water kept out the air, so they didn't rot. Dinosaurs weren't marine creatures, but some of them did live in bogs or by rivers and lakes. Some of these dinosaurs got covered in silt and turned into fossils.

Become a fossil-finder!

Look in areas where other people have found fossils before. You might well be rewarded with a fossil find of your own.

Stay safe, away from crumbling cliffs!

Look for any stone that looks different from others.

Use a brush to clear dust from your fossil.

Check your finds online or in a fossil guidebook.

i-SPY

fossils and rocks

SPY IT! SCORE IT!

Chapter 4
Different kinds of dinosaur

Dinosaurs lived on Earth for more than 170 million years. It's hard to even think about how long a stretch of time 170 million years is. And all that long, long time, the Earth was constantly changing. In fact, it's still changing now.

Nyasasaurus parringtoni may be the first known dinosaur. It's about 243 million years old.

Do you like its fluffy head? If only they'd called it Tufty, it would be a lot easier to read and remember!

When the Nyasasaurus parringtoni was alive, there was just one great lump of land on Earth, surrounded by sea. All the countries and continents we know now were part of that big land mass. People now call that huge land Pangea.

About 195 million years ago, Pangea began to break up. It happened so slowly that you wouldn't notice it happening. Chunks of land broke away from the big land mass. Very slowly, they started to move around the Earth.

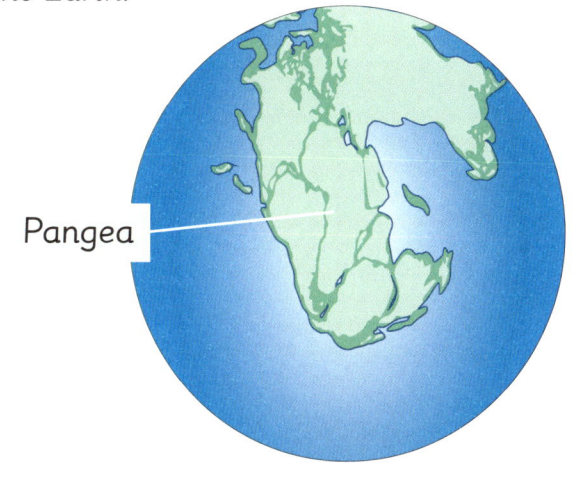

Pangea

As those chunks of land moved to new places, they began to change. Some areas of land got hotter or colder. Some areas of land got dryer or wetter. All those changes affected the dinosaurs that lived in these places. The dinosaurs had to change too, in order to carry on living there. These changes took millions of years.

It wasn't just the dinosaurs that were changing. Plants changed, too. And new creatures developed.

Did you know?
Britain wasn't an island until long after the dinosaurs had gone.

By the end of the time of the dinosaurs, they were living alongside the first snakes, flowers and bees. There were conifer trees, monkey puzzle trees and ferns. In fact, quite a lot of plants you might know began life during the time of the dinosaurs. Look in your local park or garden, and you might see trees that dinosaurs would recognise, from evergreen pines to flowering magnolias.

Different sizes and shapes of dinosaur suited different places and ways of life.

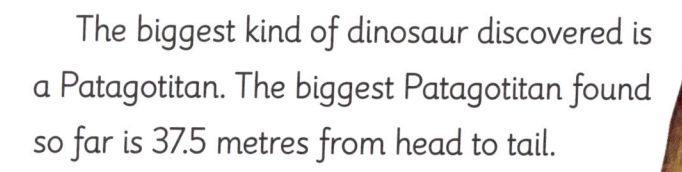

The biggest kind of dinosaur discovered is a Patagotitan. The biggest Patagotitan found so far is 37.5 metres from head to tail.

Patagotitans lived about 101 million years ago. We know from their flat teeth that they were plant eaters.

Having such a long neck let the Patagotitan reach plants that other animals couldn't reach. Their bodies were huge, but their brains were only about as big as an apple!

life-sized model of a Patagotitan with real people

The smallest dinosaurs found so far are Microraptors.

microraptor

They were about the size of chickens and walked on two legs. They had feathered arms that were almost like wings. Because they looked so much like birds, experts think that these little dinosaurs **evolved** into the birds we see today. Various things distinguish those dinosaur birds from modern birds. For one thing, the dinosaur birds had teeth!

Polacanthus dinosaurs had hard shield plates and spikes. Experts think that was probably to guard against predator bites.

Polacanthus

A Stegosaurus is easy to identify because of the hard petal shaped plates sticking up on its back. Were the plates a kind of shield to protect the Stegosaurus? Were they for receiving and storing warmth from sunlight, as if they were solar panels? Or was the Stegosaurus's strong physique just to make it look scary?

> Maybe the Stegosaurus's physique had a purpose that experts haven't even guessed at yet …

We know from their teeth that the only food eaten by Stegosaurus and Polacanthus dinosaurs was plants. We can therefore guess that the spikes were not intended for attacking others.

In contrast, some of the meat-eating dinosaurs looked quite cuddly! Some had fluffy feathers on their bodies for warmth. This Sinosauropteryx was found in China, complete with remains of feathers. Black and beige feathers also gave this dinosaur **camouflage**. That made it harder for the animals it was hunting to see it coming.

The Sinosauropteryx ran on two back legs and had short arms with thumbs to help it seize small animals such as lizards.

BONUS
Be a footprint detective

Can you match the footprints to the dinosaur description?

1 T-rex 
Three-toed tracks one after the other a wide distance apart. This shows a large meat-eating dinosaur that walked on two legs.

2 Velociraptor 
Two-toed tracks with a short distance between each step. This shows a smaller dinosaur that held one sharp claw off the ground.

3 Apatosaurus 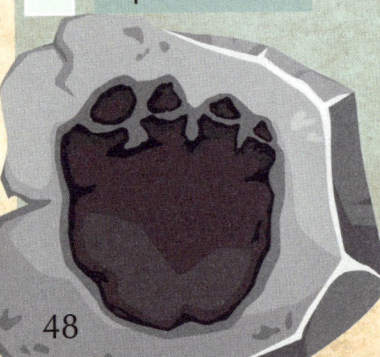
Parallel tracks that sank deep into mud. This shows a big, heavy dinosaur that walked on four legs.

49

Chapter 5
When and why did dinosaurs die out?

Experts think that birds are the only present-day **descendants** from dinosaurs.

Why are birds the only dinosaur survivors? What ended most dinosaurs' time on Earth after they had lived here for so very many millions of years?

This cassowary bird can't fly, and it does look similar to some dinosaurs. It's not hard to believe it's related to them!

It feels strange that this tiny bee hummingbird is a living descendant from dinosaurs!

Experts have worked out that most dinosaurs became extinct 66 million years ago. But how did this happen? Did they all get ill with some disease, perhaps? That's unlikely, because whatever killed the dinosaurs also killed marine creatures such as ichthyosaurs. What kind of disease could kill creatures on land and in the sea all around the world at the same time? It would have to be something catastrophic.

66 million years ago an enormous **asteroid** from space crashed into Earth. The asteroid must have hit Earth so hard that it destroyed most living things.

A vast **crater** has been found on the sea floor near Mexico. Experts think that an asteroid about ten kilometers wide crashed into the sea. The asteroid made an enormous crater on the floor of the sea, 150 kilometers wide. Think about the splash and shudder when that gigantic asteroid landed!

This is how that event might have looked.

The asteroid instantly killed any creatures that were living near where it landed.

But how could it have killed creatures all around the world?

When the asteroid hit the sea, it made massive waves that washed over a lot of land. Those waves would have drowned many plants and animals.

The asteroid crash also made volcanoes erupt, spewing out lava and dust and poisonous gases. No dinosaurs or plants would have survived the touch of hot lava. Dust and poisonous gases in the air would have made it difficult for creatures to breathe. Those poisonous gases travelled all around the world.

Experts think that more creatures died from not being able to breathe than from being hit by the asteroid.

Dust from volcanoes and smoke from fires made the sky dark, blocking out the sunshine. Plants need sunlight to grow, so many died. With not many plants to eat, plant-eating dinosaurs starved to death. When those dinosaurs died, there were fewer animals for the meat-eating dinosaurs to eat, so they died from starvation too.

Ash in the air stopped warmth and light from the sun reaching Earth's surface. Experts think that the world became cold at that time, and that sudden cold would have killed even more plants and animals.

But how did the smallest kinds of dinosaurs survive when all the big ones died? Maybe they survived by eating insects?

Experts believe that, altogether, about three-quarters of all life on Earth died at that time.

But the earthquakes, huge waves and volcanic eruptions were good for making fossils. Dead creatures would have been covered in mud, ash or silt. In the millions of years after the asteroid hit Earth, those creatures became fossils.

Over time, clean air and sunlight returned to the world. Because nearly all the large predators had been destroyed, the smaller creatures thrived once clean air and sunlight had returned.

The only large predator left wasn't a dinosaur. It was the crocodile. Maybe crocodiles survived because they can live for up to a year without eating?

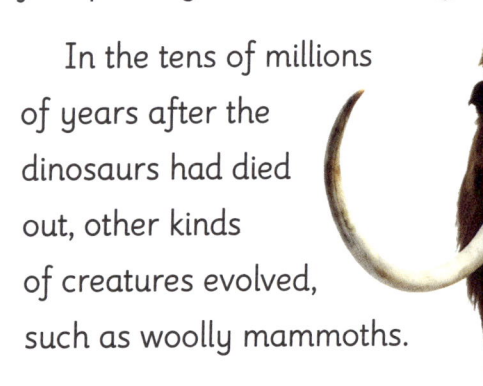

In the tens of millions of years after the dinosaurs had died out, other kinds of creatures evolved, such as woolly mammoths.

But woolly mammoths became extinct about 4,000 years ago. Why? Partly because, in the last two million years, humans have evolved. Humans were a new predator, learning to kill mammoths for their meat, skin and tusks. We made and used weapons that let us kill creatures bigger than ourselves.

This is a cave painting, tens of thousands of years old.

If dinosaurs hadn't died out, Earth might look very different today. It's interesting to think about that!

Chapter 6

Can we bring dinosaurs back?

Could we ever bring dinosaurs back to life?

Experts have found a way to make copies of animals by using the animals' DNA. This technique is called 'cloning'. DNA is a unique code that every living thing has in every part of their body – including humans.

> Here is human DNA under a very strong microscope.

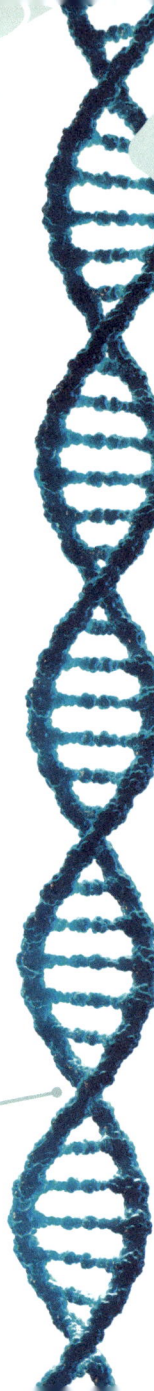

In 1996, scientists used sheep DNA to create the world's first cloned animal – a lamb called Dolly. Dolly was an exact copy of the sheep whose DNA had been used to make her.

Could scientists clone a dinosaur?

They would need to find some dinosaur DNA. DNA has been found in woolly mammoth fossils, but never in fossils that are 66 million years old like dinosaur fossils.

But could dinosaur DNA have been preserved some other way? Frozen woolly mammoths have been found, preserved for thousands of years. Just as a freezer preserves food, frozen dead animals hardly decay at all. This baby mammoth was dug from frozen ground. She was only a month old when she died 42,000 years ago!

The baby mammoth has been named Lyuba.

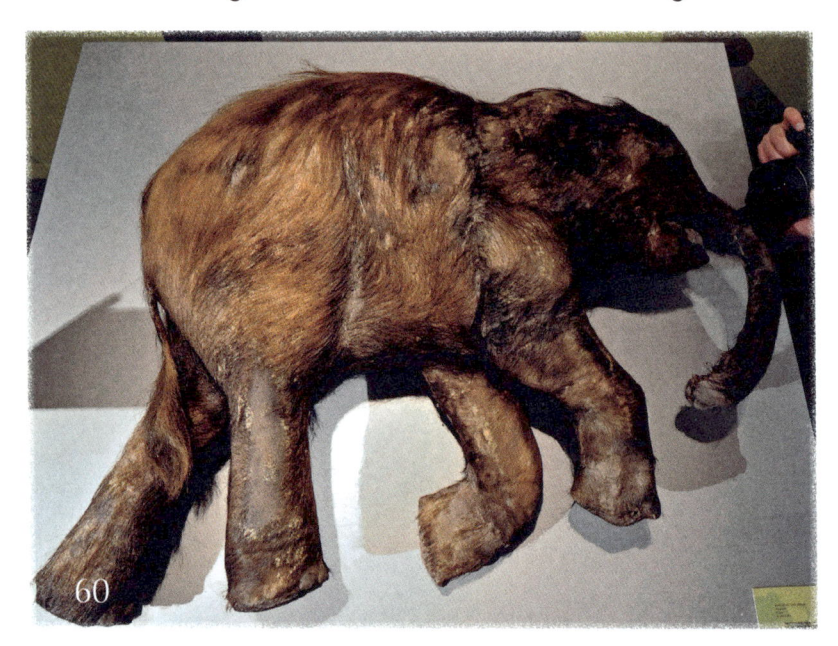

Scientists are trying to extract DNA from the baby mammoth. They plan to mix her DNA with a modern-day elephant to make a 'mammophant'.

Scientists can use Lyuba's DNA for experiments, because her DNA was preserved when she was frozen. But dinosaurs lived much longer ago than woolly mammoths. Nowhere on Earth has stayed frozen for all of the last 66 million years, since the time of the dinosaurs. So there is no chance of finding frozen dinosaur DNA.

Some people thought that dinosaur DNA might have survived in amber, just as that feather and tick did.

Because amber is see-through, you can sometimes see interesting things in it.

Fleas lived at the same time as dinosaurs. If fleas bit dinosaurs' veins, might there be dinosaur DNA inside a flea trapped in amber?

This 20-million-year-old flea was trapped in amber, but that was long after the dinosaurs had died out.

Can you see the flea trapped in this amber?

Scientists have discovered that even if dinosaur DNA was ever found, it wouldn't work to clone a new baby dinosaur. Even frozen DNA stops working after about one million years.

But there is a technique which just might get one kind of dinosaur back. Maybe scientists could select the modern birds that are most like dinosaurs, to be parents to baby birds. Then they could select the most dinosaur-like baby birds to be the next parents, and so on. Each time they did this, the baby birds would look more like a dinosaur bird than the ones before, until finally they got to a dinosaur bird.

Could that technique give us a dinosaur? It would have to be repeated many millions of times for it to work.

Even if we could bring dinosaurs back, should we do it?

If we made a dinosaur, what kind of life would it have? What kind of danger might it put people in? Earth is so different from how it was tens of millions of years ago. Would the dinosaur have to live in some kind of safari park, fed by people? It couldn't live a proper dinosaur kind of life.

Many people feel that we should spend our time and money in saving and protecting the animals we have on Earth now. A scary number of plants and creatures will become extinct unless we save them.

65

Here's one example. A kind of rhino called a northern white rhino has very nearly died out. There are only two left in the world, and both of them are female. They can't have babies without a male. So, when these two last rhinos die, northern white rhinos will be extinct. But there is hope.

Scientists want to use DNA from northern white rhinos to create new baby rhinos. Let's hope that technique works!

Are you sad that you won't ever see a living dinosaur? Perhaps you can have fun, bringing them to life in pictures and stories!

Glossary

asteroid a lump of rock in space

camouflage colouring that hides something

continents large sections of land: on Earth there are seven

crater a bowl-shaped hole where something has hit or exploded

descendants the children, grandchildren and great-grandchildren, and so on, of a person or animal (like a family tree)

evolved changed or developed slowly and gradually

extinct died out

marine in or from the sea

preserved kept as it was, not damaged or decayed

resin brown sticky liquid from trees

silt sand, soil or mud in a river

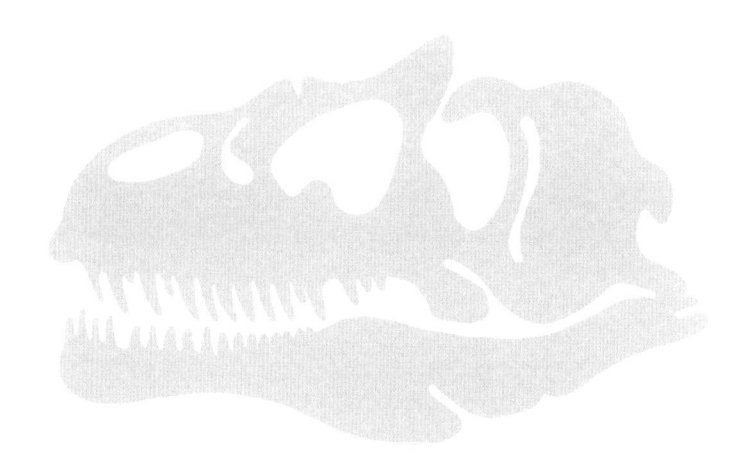

About the author

Why did you want to be a writer?

I didn't! At least, I didn't when I was a child. I found reading and writing very hard, so I never thought that anybody would pay me to do those things. But I've always loved stories, and writing is a wonderful way to get a story made and saved and shared. I absolutely love writing now.

Pippa Goodhart

How do you write an information book like this?

I had to do quite a lot of finding out about dinosaurs before I could write about them. It was really interesting learning lots from books and online and in museums. I wrote about the things I had discovered that most interested me. I hope they interest you too!

What's it like for you to write?

If I have ideas and time and know what I want to say, then writing is fun. Often new ideas pop into my head as I write. But writing can also be hard. Perhaps those hard writing times make it all the more pleasing when it comes right in the end?

Where do you like to write?

I'm very lucky that I now have my Dad's old desk to work at, and a room that's just for work. We built our own house, and I wanted a place where I could leave my messy work out and come back to it without having to clear it all away each time. But I work just about anywhere, on trains and in cafes, and of course just in my head!

What's the most interesting thing you learnt when writing this book?

There was so much that I learnt! I learnt that dinosaur fossils made people think there used to be giant humans. And I learnt that dinosaurs had feathers and changed over millions of years to be birds like my own pet chickens! Now I look at pictures of dinosaurs and see that so many artists get that wrong!

What do you hope readers will get out of the book?

I hope that you will learn interesting things about our planet's past. I hope that this book makes you think about our planet's future. And I hope that it makes you realise how important children can be in making discoveries.

Have you ever found a fossil?

Yes! I used to find marine fossils they call 'devil's toenails' in the gravel near my house. But I have also walked along chalk cliffs in France and found quite big ammonites. No dinosaur ... yet!

Book chat

What did you know about dinosaurs before reading this book?

What have you learnt from reading this book?

What's been the most interesting thing for you in this book?

Have you ever seen or found a fossil?

Where do you like to write?

I'm very lucky that I now have my Dad's old desk to work at, and a room that's just for work. We built our own house, and I wanted a place where I could leave my messy work out and come back to it without having to clear it all away each time. But I work just about anywhere, on trains and in cafes, and of course just in my head!

What's the most interesting thing you learnt when writing this book?

There was so much that I learnt! I learnt that dinosaur fossils made people think there used to be giant humans. And I learnt that dinosaurs had feathers and changed over millions of years to be birds like my own pet chickens! Now I look at pictures of dinosaurs and see that so many artists get that wrong!

What do you hope readers will get out of the book?

I hope that you will learn interesting things about our planet's past. I hope that this book makes you think about our planet's future. And I hope that it makes you realise how important children can be in making discoveries.

Have you ever found a fossil?

Yes! I used to find marine fossils they call 'devil's toenails' in the gravel near my house. But I have also walked along chalk cliffs in France and found quite big ammonites. No dinosaur ... yet!

Book chat

What did you know about dinosaurs before reading this book?

What have you learnt from reading this book?

What's been the most interesting thing for you in this book?

Have you ever seen or found a fossil?

Have you ever seen any dinosaur bones in a museum?

Which type of dinosaur would be the scariest to meet?

Where might you be able to find fossils near where you live?

Would you like to go fossil hunting?

If you had to think up a new name for the book, what would it be?

If you could ask the author anything, what would you ask?

What dinosaur do you like best and why?

If you discovered a dinosaur, what would you name it?

Would you recommend this book? Why or why not?

How do you think Mary Anning felt when she found her fossil?

Book challenge:

Draw a fossil you would love to find.

Published by Collins An imprint of HarperCollins*Publishers*

The News Building
1 London Bridge Street
London
SE1 9GF
UK

Macken House
39/40 Mayor Street Upper
Dublin 1
D01 C9W8
Ireland

© HarperCollins*Publishers* Limited 2024

10 9 8 7 6 5 4 3 2 1

ISBN 978-0-00-868125-8

All rights reserved. No part of this publication may be reproduced, stored in a retrieval system, or transmitted in any form by any means, electronic, mechanical, photocopying, recording or otherwise, without the prior written permission of the Publisher or a licence permitting restricted copying in the United Kingdom issued by the Copyright Licensing Agency Ltd, 5th Floor, Shackleton House, 4 Battle Bridge Lane, London SE1 2HX.

British Library Cataloguing-in-Publication Data
A catalogue record for this publication is available from the British Library.

Download the teaching notes and word cards to accompany this book at: http://littlewandle.org.uk/signupfluency/

Get the latest Collins Big Cat news at
collins.co.uk/collinsbigcat

Author: Pippa Goodhart
Illustrator: Caitlin O'Dwyer (Astound Illustration Agency)
Publisher: Laura White
Product manager: Caroline Green
Series editor: Charlotte Raby
Development editor: Catherine Baker
Commissioning editor: Suzannah Ditchburn
Project manager: Emily Hooton
Copyeditor: Sally Byford
Image researcher: Sophie Hartley
Proofreader: Catherine Dakin
Cover designer: Sarah Finan
Typesetter: 2Hoots Publishing Services Ltd
Production controller: Katharine Willard

Printed in the UK.

MIX
Paper | Supporting responsible forestry
FSC™ C007454

This book is produced from independently certified FSC™ paper to ensure responsible forest management.

For more information visit: www.harpercollins.co.uk/green

Made with responsibly sourced paper and vegetable ink

Scan to see how we are reducing our environmental impact.

Acknowledgements
The publishers gratefully acknowledge the permission granted to reproduce the copyright material in this book. Every effort has been made to trace copyright holders and to obtain their permission for the use of copyright material. The publishers will gladly receive any information enabling them to rectify any error or omission at the first opportunity.

p3t Universal Images Group North America LLC/DeAgostini/Alamy, p3cl Julius T Csotonyi/Science Photo Library, p3c Sebastian Kaulitzki/Science Photo Library, p3bl David Gifford/Science Photo Library, p3bc Aunt Spray/Alamy, p6t Millard H. Sharp/Science Source/Science Photo Library, p6b Aunt Spray/Alamy, p7t Ivy Close Images/Alamy, p7b Paul D Stewart/Science Photo Library, p8 David Robinson/Alamy, p10 Granger - Historical Picture Archive/Alamy, p13b Daniel Eskridge/Shutterstock, p14 IanDagnall Computing/Alamy, p16 Granger - Historical Picture Archive/Alamy, p17t Adrian Chinery/Alamy, p19 tony french/Alamy, p24l Mikkel Juul Jensen/Science Photo Library, p24r Sebastian Kaulitzkis/Science Photo Library, p25 Jose Antonio Peñas/Science Photo Library, p26t Stocktrek Images, Inc./Alamy, p26b Julius T Csotonyi/Science Photo Library, p27b Sergey Krasovskiy/Stocktrek Images/Getty Images, p28b 2021 China News Service/Getty Images, p29 Creative Commons Attribution License, p32 John Cancalosi/Alamy, p33r Jim Lane/Alamy, p34 Wales News Service, p35 Corbin17/Alamy, p36 Peñalver, E., Arillo, A., Delclòs, X. et al. Nat Commun 8, 1924 (2017), p38c geogphotos/Alamy, p38b Christina Bollen/Alamy, p39c Courtesy of HarperCollins*Publishers*, p40 Science Photo Library/Alamy, p47r Toronto Star/Getty Images, p48 Anzhela Buch/Alamy, p49t Biosphoto/Alamy, p49c Maxime Dube/Alamy, p49b Interfoto/Alamy, p51 Kike Calvo/Alamy, p57 Universal History Archive/Bridgeman Images, p59 Karen Kasmauski, p60 Associated Press/Alamy, p62 K. H. Kjeldsen/Science Photo Library, p66 Dmytro Pylypenko/Alamy. All other images, Shutterstock.

Thank you to Lily Wilder and her family for details about her fossil find.